Celebrating American Heroes

Celebrating American Heroes

Plays for Students of English

STUDENT PLAY BOOK

Anne Siebert

with illustrations by Marilynne K. Roach

Pro Lingua Associates

Pro Lingua Associates, Publishers
P.O. Box 1348
Brattleboro, Vermont 05302 USA
Office: 802 257 7779
Orders: 800 366 4775
E-mail: prolingu@sover.net
Webstore: www.ProLinguaAssociates.com
SAN: 216-0579

At Pro Lingua
our objective is to foster an approach
to learning and teaching that we call
Interplay, *the* **inter***action of language*
learners and teachers with their materials,
with the language and culture,
and with each other in active, creative,
and productive **play**.

Copyright © 2000 by Anne Siebert
ISBN 0-86647-127-8

This book was designed by Arthur A. Burrows and Judith Ashkenaz, It was set in
11/14 Electra with Apple Chancery display type in Brattleboro, Vermont, and it
was printed and bound by Sheridan Books of Fredericksburg, Virginia.

The illustrations are by Marilynne K. Roach

Printed in the United States of America
Second printing 2000: 3500 copies in print.

Also available: **Celebrating American Heroes: Teacher's Guide**

Contents

For Emily, Laura, Matthew, and Mark

Making the First American Flag

Betsy Ross
1752–1836

George Washington
1732–1799

No one knows for certain how and when the first American flag was made. However, it is possible that General George Washington asked Betsy Ross to make one when he visited her in 1776.

Betsy Ross and George Washington

Making the First American Flag

Cast: Narrator
General George Washington
Aide to General Washington
Betsy Ross
Chorus

Narrator: This is a legend, a story of how Americans got their first flag. It takes place in Philadelphia. The year is 1776. At that time there was no American flag. There was only the British flag because America was a British colony. So, when the colonists fought the British, they needed their own flag. Here is what happened. General Washington is talking to his aide.

Washington: Our soldiers are fighting the British. They are brave soldiers, good soldiers, but we have a problem, a big problem. We have no flag. We have only the British flag. We need an American flag for them and for our nation.

Aide: You're right, General Washington. We do need an American flag. But who could make this new flag? Who could do it? Where could we get it?

CHORUS: *Betsy Ross!*
Betsy Ross!
You must go
To Betsy Ross!

Washington: Betsy Ross? Who is Betsy Ross?

CHORUS: *A seamstress!*
A seamstress!
A very famous
Seamstress.

Aide: That's right, General. Betsy Ross is a very famous seamstress. She can sew a flag. She can sew an American flag. And she lives right here in Philadelphia.

Washington: Then, let's go. Let's go and see her. Let's go right now! We really need a flag! We need a flag for this new country.

CHORUS: *Of course, of course!*
We need a flag.
We need a flag
For what we stand for:
For freedom and justice
For everyone!

Narrator: It's evening, and Betsy Ross is busy sewing. There is a knock at the door.

Betsy Ross: I wonder who that can be at this time of night. It's late!

Washington: Good evening, madam. I am General George Washington. Is this the home of Betsy Ross?

Betsy Ross: Yes, General Washington! Yes! I am Betsy Ross. Please come in. It's such an honor to have you in our home! Please sit down. May I bring you something?

Washington: No, thank you, madam. I am here on very important business. As you know, our brave soldiers are fighting. It's a terrible, terrible fight.

Betsy Ross: Yes, of course. I know, but what can I do? How can I help?

Washington: Dear lady, our men have no flag. They need a flag! This country needs a flag. We need a flag to show that we are a nation. We need a flag to show what we stand for. Could you make such a flag for us?

CHORUS: *Betsy, Betsy!*
Make that flag.
Make it a symbol
Of this land.
A new land, a free land!

Betsy Ross: Of course, General Washington. I'll be happy to make that flag. It will be my honor. But what will be on it? How will I make it?

Washington: Hmm. Let's see. First, we must have thirteen white stars for the thirteen states. Then we must have thirteen stripes. And the colors should be red, white, and blue. Can you do it? Can you make the flag? We need it very much. We need it soon!

Betsy Ross: General Washington, I'll get to it immediately. I'll do it for our brave soldiers and our brave country. I'll get to work right away. There isn't much time!

Washington: Good night, dear lady! I shall return soon!

Betsy Ross: Good night, General Washington. Thank you for your visit.

CHORUS: *She worked all day.*
She worked at night.
Sewing, sewing,
The very first flag,
The very first flag
Of this land!

Narrator: A few days later, there is a knock on the door.

Betsy Ross: General Washington! Please come in! I have something for you. The flag is finished. Let me show it to you! I hope you like it!

Washington: Ah! Madam, it's beautiful! It's the most beautiful flag in the world. You have made a wonderful flag. You have done a wonderful service to this country. I thank you, and the country thanks you!

CHORUS: *So it was, so it was*
Betsy Ross sewed a flag,
A new flag, a proud flag
For this land!
A new flag, a proud flag
For this land!

Narrator: On June 14, 1777, this flag, also called the Stars and Stripes, became the official flag of the United States. Today it flies over the White House and other important buildings with *fifty* stars and thirteen stripes.

Don't Burn the White House!

Dolley Madison
1768–1849

During the War of 1812, the British invaded Washington, D.C. They set fire to the president's house. Dolley Madison, wife of the fourth U.S. president, James Madison, saved George Washington's portrait and many documents just minutes before the British burned the White House.

Dolley Madison

Don't Burn the White House!

Cast: *Narrator*
Dolley Madison
Messenger
Chorus

Narrator: The White House, where the president lives, is a very special and important place because it is a symbol of freedom and democracy. We are going to learn a little bit about the White House — its history, how it almost burned down, and how it got its name.

CHORUS: *The White House is*
A special place.
It belongs to you,
It belongs to me.
It is a symbol
Of democracy!

Narrator: This story is about a First Lady, Dolley Madison. She was the wife of the fourth president of the United States, James Madison. She was a very special and popular First Lady. She was an excellent hostess, known for her kindness and tact. She was also very brave. It is 1812, and the U.S. is at war with Britain.

CHORUS: *Dolley, Dolley,*
What did you?
What did you do
that was so brave?

Dolley: Well, I don't really think I was that brave. Let me explain. We were at war with Britain, and they were invading the capital! They were coming to the White House! I couldn't believe that! I couldn't believe that they might burn it down — this beautiful house where we had many wonderful parties and ceremonies.

CHORUS: *Dolley, Dolley,*
What did you do?
What did you do
That special day?

Dolley: Well, at first, I did nothing. I was having supper, and I heard cannons in the distance! It couldn't be! The British couldn't be in Washington! I had not finished eating when I heard a knock on the door.

Messenger: Madam, this is a message from your husband, the president! He wants you to leave Washington at once! He wants you to go to Virginia, where it is safe! You will not be safe if you stay here!

Dolley: No, I'll wait for the president! I'll wait right here. I'll wait until he comes. I will not leave alone. We will leave together!

Messenger: Madam, I beg you. Leave! Leave at once. There is no time! The president cannot come. Don't you hear the cannons? The British are near!

CHORUS: *The British are coming!*
The British are coming!

Messenger: They'll capture you!

Dolley: Then I must go at once. Please get me a carriage, for I have much to pack.

Messenger: Madam! Don't wait another minute. Don't pack too much. Don't take too long!

CHORUS: *Dolley, Dolley,*
What did you pack?
What did you pack?
On the run?
On the run?

Dolley: I thought about all the documents in the White House. I had to take them. They were treasures, national treasures! I wanted to take as many as I could. I couldn't leave without them. The Declaration of Independence, for example — I had to take that and other documents, too.

CHORUS: *Did you leave*
Right then?
Did you leave
Right there?
When did you leave?
When did you leave?

Dolley: Not right away. I saw that wonderful portrait of George Washington on the wall and thought, "I cannot leave without it!" So, I told my servants to take it down and to cut it out of the frame.

Messenger: Madam, please! Please! The president insists that you leave at once! The British are almost at your doorstep! Go! Now! Before it is too late.

CHORUS: *Go, Dolley, go!*
Go, Dolley, go!
Go to a safe place
Before it gets too late!

Dolley: Yes, yes, I'm leaving. I pray the British do not destroy this beautiful home.

Narrator: And so she left quickly, with treasures in hand and dinner still warm on the table. The British arrived, ate the food, and then set fire to the house. After the Americans turned back the British, the president and Dolley returned to the White House. It was now gray with the burn marks of the fire. But it was still there!

CHORUS: *How sad, how sad,*
To burn it down.
How sad, how sad,
To burn it down!
The house so white,
But now so gray.

Narrator: Well, the house was restored and painted white once again. Soon after, people began calling it the White House. Then, in 1902, President Theodore Roosevelt made it official: it was to be called the "White House" from then on.

CHORUS: *The White House is*
A very special place.
In this place
The president lives.
In this place
The president works.
His house, our house,
Everybody's house!
The White House is
A very special place!

Narrator: The White House is truly a national treasure, and so are the things Dolley Madison saved.

Crossing the Continent to the Pacific

Sacagawea
1787?–1812?

Many years ago, much of America's land was wild, unknown, and dangerous. In 1804, President Thomas Jefferson asked Lewis and Clark to explore it. Sacagawea was a young Indian woman who was their guide, interpreter, and an important member of the expedition. Without her, Lewis and Clark might never have reached the Pacific Ocean.

Sacagawea

Crossing the Continent to the Pacific

Cast: Narrator
Sacagawea, Indian guide and interpreter
Meriwether Lewis, explorer
William Clark, explorer
Cameahwait, Indian Chief
Chorus

Narrator: The year is 1804. The United States has just bought land from France, and President Thomas Jefferson wants to explore it. The land is huge, wild, unknown, and dangerous. He asks Lewis and Clark to lead an expedition.

CHORUS: *And so they went,*
And so they went,
Exploring, exploring
The unknown land.
Exploring, exploring
The unknown land.

Narrator: Travel was not easy. When winter came, they set up camp in an Indian village and waited until spring to travel again. They did not know the way. Who would help them? One day, an Indian woman came to the camp with her husband. Her name was Sacagawea.

CHORUS: *Sacagawea!*
Sacagawea!
What is your story?
Tell us your story.
Please tell us
About yourself.

Sacagawea: I am a Shoshone. My family were nomads. We traveled from place to place. When I was eleven, another Indian tribe attacked my village, and I was kidnapped. I learned the languages of many Indian tribes.

CHORUS: *How awful!*
How awful!
How very, very awful!
What happened then?
What happened then,
Sacagawea?
What happened then?

Sacagawea: After about four years, they sold me to this man, Charbonneau. He became my husband. And this is my baby, just four months old.

Lewis: Sacagawea, can you come with us? Can you come on this expedition? We need a guide. We need someone who can be an interpreter. We need someone who knows the land and these languages. Can you come?

Sacagawea: Yes, yes, I would be happy to come. My husband and I will go with you.

CHORUS: *And so she went,*
And so she went,
With a baby
On her back,
With a baby
On her back,
Guiding, helping
Along the way.

Narrator: One day, the boat she was in came upon rough waters. It almost sank. Valuable things started to float away. Everybody panicked except Sacagawea. She saved all the valuable goods.

CHORUS: *Sacagawea!*
Sacagawea!
You saved the day!
You saved the day!
Thanks to you,
Little was lost.
Sacagawea,
You saved the day!

Narrator Then, later in the voyage, something very unusual happened. Sacagawea, Lewis, and Clark came to an Indian village. As Sacagawea approached the Indian village, she stopped. She couldn't believe her eyes. Could it be? Was it possible? Was it really possible?

CHORUS: *Sacagawea,*
It is true.
This is your home
Of long ago.
Sacagawea,
Sacagawea,
Welcome home!
Welcome home!

Sacagawea: And these are my people! Look, there's my friend, my beautiful friend. But they say my sister is gone! She's dead! But I am happy to be among my people again! I am home again! I am home!

Clark: Sacagawea, the chief has called a council meeting. Let us go and meet him. You can interpret for us. These are your people.

CHORUS: *And so they sat*
Inside a tent.
Cameahwait,
The Indian Chief,
Began to speak,
Began to speak.

Sacagawea: Cameahwait! Cameahwait! Is it you? I don't believe it! I can't believe it! Don't you know me, Cameahwait? I am Sacagawea. I'm your sister! Your sister!

Cameahwait: My sister! My beloved sister! My sister who was kidnapped! My sister who was lost is here! We are together again. Do not cry, dear sister!

Sacagawea: These are tears of joy, my brother. These are tears of joy for meeting my brother again. At last! We are together again.

Cameahwait: Come, sister, let us talk. Let's talk of days gone by.

Narrator: And so Sacagawea told her brother about the years gone by. She also explained that Lewis and Clark were friendly.

Lewis: We need horses to get across the mountains.

Clark: Cameahwait, can you help us? Can you give us horses?

Cameahwait: Yes, we can help. We will give you the horses you need. But, Sacagawea, my sister, will you stay with us? Can you return to your people?

Sacagawea: No, my brother, I cannot stay. I have a new life. I have a husband. I have a child. I have learned new ways. I cannot stay. I will help my new friends. And I, too, want to see the great ocean. Goodbye, my brother.

Cameahwait: Goodbye, my dear sister, 'til we meet again.

CHORUS: *Sacagawea, Sacagawea,*
Your old life is gone.
Your old life is gone.
Gone like the wind,
Gone like the wind.
Your new life is here,
Exploring the land.

Narrator: And so, on November 7, 1805, after a long, hard journey across the wide plains and the high mountains, Lewis and Clark reached the Pacific Ocean, thanks in great part to Sacagawea, the quiet, brave woman who helped them so much as a guide, interpreter, and friend.

The Little Woman Who Started the Big War

Harriet Beecher Stowe
1811–1896

In 1852, Harriet Beecher Stowe wrote a powerful anti-slavery book, Uncle Tom's Cabin. *It was an immediate best-seller. In addition to raising seven children, Harriet Beecher Stowe wrote books, gave speeches, and had an important meeting with President Abraham Lincoln.*

Harriet Beecher Stowe

The Little Woman Who Started the Big War

Cast: Narrator
Harriet Beecher Stowe
President Abraham Lincoln
Isabella, Harriet's sister-in-law
Henry Ward, Harriet's brother
Calvin Stowe, Harriet's husband
Chorus

Narrator: The year is 1852. There is a huge conflict in the country. In the South, black people are not free. They are slaves. The states in the North say this is wrong and must not continue. Harriet Beecher Stowe, a housewife with seven children, writes a very famous book about this situation.

CHORUS: *Mrs. Stowe, Mrs. Stowe,*
How did you feel?
How did you feel
About this evil
Situation?

Harriet: Oh, I was really angry and upset. Slavery was wrong! Very wrong! I wanted to speak out against it. Many men in the North were speaking out against it. I wanted to speak out against it, too. I wanted to *do* something.

Isabella: Listen, Harriet, you are a writer. Write about slavery. Make this country listen to your words. This country needs to see how terrible slavery is. You should write about it.

Harriet: You're right. But, this slavery problem — isn't that a job for a man? What will my husband say? What will my father think? And my brothers, what will they think? I don't want to go against my family. Sometimes I wish I were a man.

Narrator: Then, one day, she was talking to her brother.

Henry: So, dear sister, you want to write about slavery. That's an excellent idea! Do it, Harriet! Do it! You should speak about this cause. You have got to speak out against slavery as I do.

Harriet: Thank you, Henry, but right now I don't know how to begin or where to begin. I'll have to think about it. I really have to think about it.

Narrator: Then, on one cold February morning, while Harriet was in church, something happened.

CHORUS: *It came to her,*
It came to her,
The story she would write
Came to her.
She had a vision,
A clear, clear vision
Of what she would write,
Of what she would say.

Harriet: That's true. The story came to me — all at once. I had a vision. I saw Tom, the slave, and the master, and even Little Eliza. I saw them all. I heard them speak. I couldn't wait to get home and write.

CHORUS: *She wrote and wrote,*
She didn't stop.
Often with
A child on her lap,
She wrote it all,
She didn't stop.
She didn't stop
Until she finished.

Narrator: One day, Calvin read her manuscript.

Calvin: Harriet! This is excellent! This story is wonderful! The people are real and alive. You should send it in for publication.

Harriet: And that's what I did. I sent it to a newspaper. It published the stories week by week, as a serial.

Narrator: So every week, the next part of the story appeared. Readers loved it. And the stories just grew and grew!

CHORUS: *Week by week*
They would wait.
They would wait
For what happened next
To Uncle Tom,
To Simon Legree,
To runaway Eliza.

Narrator: Finally, on March 20, 1852, *Uncle Tom's Cabin* was published as a book. It was a huge success, a best-seller, both in America and in England. With one small book, Harriet Beecher Stowe had fired up a nation on the problem of slavery.

CHORUS: *It made people sad!*
It made people mad!
Uncle Tom's Cabin
Made them mad!

Narrator: Then, in 1861, the Civil War broke out. Harriet traveled and lectured. She became famous. One day, she went to the White House to speak with President Lincoln.

Lincoln: Welcome to the White House, Mrs. Stowe! So you're the little lady who started the big war!

Harriet: Oh, Mr. President, I did what I could. But our work isn't finished, Mr. President. Black people are not yet free. They must be free!

Lincoln: Yes, dear lady. They must be free. I have here a new document, the Emancipation Proclamation. It will give Negroes their freedom. I will sign it soon.

Harriet: Oh, thank you, Mr. Lincoln! Yes, sign it soon. It will mean a lot for our country.

Narrator: And on January 1, 1863, President Lincoln signed the Emancipation Proclamation. That evening, Harriet Beecher Stowe was at a concert. An announcement was made: "The Emancipation Proclamation has just been signed!"

CHORUS: *The crowd went wild!*
Everybody cheered!
They clapped!
They waved!
They stood on chairs!

Narrator: Then they saw Mrs. Stowe. And they began to cheer for her, too.

CHORUS: *Mrs. Stowe! Mrs. Stowe!*
Thank you, thank you, Mrs. Stowe.
We also cheer for you, Mrs. Stowe!

Harriet: What a night that was! It was wonderful! The war wasn't over, but we knew that Mr. Lincoln would show us the way — and he did.

Words for a Broken Nation: The Gettysburg Address

Abraham Lincoln
1809–1865

On November 19, 1863, President Lincoln gave one of the most famous speeches in history, the Gettysburg Address. This speech honored the men who died in the Battle of Gettysburg during America's Civil War. The phrase "government of the people, by the people, and for the people" comes from that speech.

Abraham Lincoln

Words for a Broken Nation: The Gettysburg Address

Cast: Narrator
President Abraham Lincoln
Edward Everett, speaker at Gettysburg
Woman
First Man
Second Man
Chorus

Narrator: It is July 1, 1863. The place is Gettysburg, Pennsylvania. The country is at war. It is America's Civil War. The North and the South have just fought a terrible battle. The North won this battle, but at a terrible price.

Lincoln: It was terrible, terrible! The North lost 18,000 men and the South 20,000. Perhaps the war will soon be over and the union saved. But now, we must bury the dead.

Narrator: And so it was decided to make Gettysburg a national cemetery, a place to bury the dead. A ceremony was planned for November 19, 1863.

Everett: I was asked to be the main speaker at this ceremony. I had been secretary of state, ambassador, and now president of Harvard University. I didn't know if the president would be there or not.

Lincoln: Yes, and I was also asked to come and make a few remarks. But it's true. Mr. Everett was the main speaker. He was a very famous orator. He had a deep, rich voice. People came to listen to him.

CHORUS: *And so came the day,*
That very famous day
When Lincoln spoke,
When Lincoln spoke.
What could he say?
What would he say
To heal a nation
Broken by war?

Lincoln: Well, first I wanted to pay tribute to our brave men. Then, I wanted to share a vision of America, that we are one nation, not two.

Narrator: And so Mr. Lincoln began to prepare his speech.

Lincoln: I thought very hard about it. We had fought to become one nation, free and great. Should we throw away all that? I came to Gettysburg a day early so that I could think about what to say.

Narrator: Thousands of people came to Gettysburg. A band played and people waited on the battlefield. And Mr. Lincoln came to the field riding a horse. A woman ran up to him.

Woman: Oh, Mr. President, Mr. President! May my little girl ride with you? She is so tired! May she ride with you?

Lincoln: Of course, dear lady. Come, little girl. Here, sit in front of me and we shall ride together.

Woman: Oh, thank you, Mr. President. You are so kind — so very, very kind.

Narrator: And the little girl rode with the President of the United States. There were many speeches that day. Edward Everett talked for two hours. It was a long afternoon. People were tired. President Lincoln was the last speaker.

First Man: I wonder what the President will say.

Second Man: I wonder, too. Let's listen.

Narrator: The president got up, put on his glasses, and began.

Lincoln: Four score and seven years ago
our fathers brought forth
upon this continent
a new nation,
conceived in liberty …

CHORUS: *Liberty, liberty!*
Conceived in liberty,
Our nation began
In liberty!

Lincoln: … and dedicated to the proposition
that all men are created equal.

CHORUS: *All men are equal.*
All men are equal.
Created equal!
Created equal!

Lincoln: … that this nation, under God,
shall have a new birth of freedom,
and that government of the people,
by the people, and for the people
shall not perish from the earth.

CHORUS: *A government*
Of the people,
By the people,
And for the people
Shall not perish
From the earth.

Narrator: When he finished his speech, nobody clapped or cheered.
It was such a short speech, and very few people thought it
was a great speech except for Everett and a few reporters.

Everett: Mr. President, your speech was majestic. It was beautiful. You said in two minutes what I tried to say in two hours.

Lincoln: Thank you, sir, but I don't think the people liked it. They wanted something more, something different. I believe I have failed.

Narrator: President Lincoln had not failed. He had written one of the greatest speeches of all time. But, sad to say, the people who were there did not realize it. They did not know that it was a speech not only for their time, but for all time.

The Man Who Turned Night into Day

Thomas Alva Edison
1847–1931

Thomas Edison was a world-famous inventor. In 1879, he invented the electric light bulb — an invention that changed the world. Edison got over 1,000 patents. He didn't go to school; he was self-taught. At an early age, he became hard of hearing, but nothing ever stopped him from learning, working, and inventing.

Thomas Alva Edison

The Man Who Turned Night into Day

Cast: Narrator
Thomas Edison
Mother
Teacher
Telegraph Operator
Chorus

Narrator: Thomas Edison was born in Milan, Ohio, on February 11, 1847. As a child, he wondered and asked about everything..

Thomas: Mother, what makes birds fly? Mother, why does water put out fire? Mother, why do chickens hatch? Mother, why …?

Mother: Why, why, why! Oh, Thomas, you do ask a lot of questions, don't you! Maybe when you go to school, you'll get some answers.

Narrator: And so Thomas did go to school, but it was not a happy experience. The teacher did not like Tom's questions. One day, he spoke to Tom's mother.

Teacher: Your son is not a good student. He can't sit still. He asks too many questions. He cannot concentrate. His mind is weak. There is nothing I can do with him.

Mother: Then I shall take him out of school. My son is not a bad student. My son is a bright and curious child who wants to learn everything. I will teach him myself!

CHORUS: *Teach him!*
Teach him!
Teach him at home.
Teach him everything
He wants to know.

Mother: Come, Thomas. We're going to learn. We're going to learn everything you want to know. Here, Thomas. I bought you a new book. It's a chemistry book.

Narrator: So the only formal education Thomas got was four months of school. His mother taught him at home and he taught himself for the rest of his life. That is how he got his education.

CHORUS: *He loved to read and learn.*
He loved to read and experiment.
That's what he loved
Most of all.

Thomas: But I needed money to buy more books and more things for my experiments. So I sold newspapers, candy, and sandwiches at the train station. I was about twelve years old.

Narrator: He became a newspaper boy on a train. Then one day, something terrible happened to Tom. He began to lose his hearing.

Thomas: Suddenly, I couldn't hear. Something broke inside my head and I couldn't hear. It was terrible!

CHORUS: *Thomas, Thomas,*
What did you do?
What did you do
When you could not hear?
When you could not hear!

Thomas: Well, at first it was really bad, but then it seemed that I could concentrate better. I got a lot of books from the library. I read them one by one. I read them all.

Narrator: Then, one day at work, Thomas saw a child playing on the railroad tracks. The train was coming! The child didn't see the train!

CHORUS: *Thomas, Thomas,*
Save that child!
Save that child
From the
Oncoming train!

Narrator: Quickly, without thinking, he grabbed the boy and saved him from the oncoming train.

Telegraph Operator: Oh, thank you, Thomas, thank you! You saved my son's life! How can I repay you?

Thomas: Let me work for you, and teach me how to send telegraphs. That will be thanks enough.

Narrator: So Thomas took a job in the telegraph office, learning, always learning. At home, he continued to experiment and invent. After that, he went to New York.

Thomas: I worked for a company in New York, but I wanted to be my own boss. I didn't want to work for anybody. So, in 1876 I bought some land in New Jersey and set up my own laboratory.

CHORUS: *He worked all day,*
He worked at night,
Working and testing,
Experimenting!

Mrs. Edison: Will you be home tonight for supper, dear?

Thomas: Oh, no, not tonight. Don't wait up for me. I'm going to stay at the laboratory all night to do an experiment. I've got many ideas to work on.

CHORUS: *And one by one,*
He tried them all.
He invented things
For me and you.
Amazing, amazing!
And wonderful, too!

Narrator: Thomas Edison invented a machine that could talk — the first phonograph. And the next year, he invented the electric light bulb.

Thomas: That's right! I had been working on an electric light bulb for a long time. Finally, on October 19, 1879, I tested it. It burned all day and all night. That was wonderful!

CHORUS: *A light, a light,*
An electric light!
Edison made
An electric light!

Narrator: People came from all over to see the new invention. They wanted the electric light for their own homes. They didn't want the gas lamps they had had before. They wanted the new, clean electric light.

Thomas: It was wonderful to light up homes and cities, but I had more work to do — many more things to invent — like the motion picture camera. I had so many ideas and so little time.

CHORUS: *Famous, famous*
He became,
For all the inventions
That he made.
He got awards
and honors, too,
Helping mankind
And me and you!

Narrator: He got over 1,000 patents, more than any other inventor in the world. He continued working, but at age 84, he became ill. Reporters waited for news outside his home. They knew that this famous man might die soon.

Mrs. Edison: Gentlemen, if Mr. Edison passes away, I shall turn off the lights in his room.

Narrator: On October 18, the lights went out. On the night of his funeral, people all across America turned off their lights to honor the man who had changed their world.

The Mountains
Love Mr. Muir

John Muir
1838–1914

John Muir was America's most famous naturalist. He loved nature above all things. Muir wrote many articles about nature so that others could enjoy it, too. But most important, he made sure that the wild lands of America were protected. Because of his work, Yosemite became a national park in 1890.

John Muir

The Mountains Love Mr. Muir

Cast: *Narrator*
John Muir, naturalist
John's father
President Theodore Roosevelt
Chorus

Narrator: John Muir was born in Scotland in 1838. He loved nature even when he was a little boy. He lived on a farm near the sea, and he loved to be out-of-doors.

CHORUS: *The birds and the trees*
Spoke to him.
The mountains and trees
Spoke to him.
Even the sea
Spoke to him!

John: That's true. I couldn't wait to go outside to smell the flowers and the air, to listen to the birds and the wind. I couldn't get enough of it. But I had to work hard as a little boy. I had much to do before I could go out and play.

John's father: John, come! Come and help me. Milk the cows and get the wood for the fire. And don't be slow!

John: Yes, Father, I'm coming, I'm coming.

Narrator: After that, he and his brother would run to the sea. They loved to be near the sea.

CHORUS: *He went to the sea,*
He went to the sea
To look, to feel,
To smell, to see
The sea, the sea,
The beautiful sea!

John: When I was eleven, we moved to America. I loved our new home in America. I loved to run in the fields with my brother. I loved to climb trees and to swim. I didn't like school. Nature was my real school.

CHORUS: *That was your school.*
Nature was your school.
Nature, nature
Was your school.
The wonder of nature
Was your school!

John: Later, I went to study at a university, but really I always wanted to be out-of-doors. Nature was my teacher. She was a good teacher, too.

CHORUS: *The trees, the trees,*
The earth, the earth.
All living things
Taught him well.
Nature, nature
Taught him well.

Narrator: One day, John had a serious accident. A piece of metal flew into his eye.

John: Oh, my God! I can't see! I can't see!

Narrator: He did get his vision back, but the accident changed him forever. He quit his job and decided to do what he loved most — study nature.

CHORUS: *He traveled here,*
He traveled there,
He traveled, traveled
Everywhere!

John: One day I arrived in California. I went to the mountains. I went to Yosemite Valley. It was beautiful! The mountains, the waterfalls, the flowers! It was the most wonderful land that I had ever seen.

CHORUS: *The mountains!*
The mountains!
The waterfalls, too!
The colorful flowers!
A wonderful view!

John: I walked up and down the mountains, everywhere. I studied the rocks and waterfalls. I studied everything. I loved it all!.

CHORUS: *You loved the wild,*
The call of the wild.
It spoke to you.
It spoke to you.
All of nature
Spoke to you.

Narrator: John wrote about Yosemite for newspapers and magazines. People enjoyed his writings. They wanted to see what he saw. One day, he asked his readers to do something very important.

John: Dear readers, please write to Congress. Please tell Congress to make Yosemite a national park. Please tell Congress to protect this land. The ranchers are destroying it. Please tell Congress to save it! We have to save it.

CHORUS: *They wrote and they wrote,*
To Congress they wrote.
Congressmen, please,
Save this land,
Save those trees!

Narrator: And in 1890, it was saved. Congress made Yosemite a National Park. John Muir became famous all over the country. He wrote thirty books and many, many articles. Famous men visited him. President Theodore Roosevelt visited him.

Roosevelt: John, remember the time I came to see you? It was wonderful, hiking in the mountains and sleeping under the stars. It was wonderful!

John: That's true. It was wonderful. And we talked all night about how to protect this beautiful wilderness.

Roosevelt: As president, I promised to do everything I could. We need to protect it so that our children and our children's children can enjoy it, too.

John Muir: That's right, Mr. President, but our fight is not over. Many people want to build on the land and destroy the trees and rivers. That is not good. This is God's country. It is the people's country.

Roosevelt: I love nature as much as you, John. I will support you in every way. Thank you for your work.

CHORUS: *Our parks, our parks,*
Our national parks
For all to see,
For all to know,
Our parks, our parks,
Our national Parks!

Narrator: Thank you, John, for all you did. All of us can now enjoy our national parks and be renewed by them. Thank you, John Muir!

The Bravest Man in Baseball

Jackie Robinson
1919–1972

In 1947, Jackie Robinson became the first black player to play on an all-white professional baseball team, the Brooklyn Dodgers. Discrimination was very strong at that time. He was hated and booed by many fans and many of the players. Jackie proved himself to be not only an excellent baseball player, but a gentleman as well.

Jackie Robinson

The Bravest Man in Baseball

Cast: Narrator
Jackie Robinson, baseball player
Branch Rickey, general manager of the Brooklyn
   Dodgers
Assistant
Pee Wee Reese, a white baseball player
Chorus

Narrator: Jackie Robinson was a black man born to a very poor family in Georgia on January 31, 1919. He was a very talented baseball player. But in the 1940s there was a big problem. There was total discrimination against blacks. Even black baseball players could not play with white players. They had to play in a different league. But Jackie Robinson was a special person. Here is his story.

CHORUS: *How sad! How sad!*
To think that a man
Could be judged
By the color,
The color of his skin.
How very, very sad!

Narrator: But everybody didn't think that way. Some believed that talent, not skin color, was the most important thing.

Branch Rickey: We have a good team right now. The Dodgers are very good, but we need to make them better. We want to win a championship. Let's take a look at the Negro League. They have some excellent players.

Assistant: They do, but if you get a black man, people may not come to the games. They'll boo him. The white players won't want to play with him, either. You're asking for a lot of trouble.

Branch: I don't care. If he's an outstanding player, it won't matter. But it's true, he will have to be a special man. He's going to be taking a lot of heat from the fans. They're going to say terrible things to him. What I need is a man of courage, someone who is strong. Think you can find someone like that?

Assistant: I don't know. I'll try. It'll be tough, but I'll try.

CHORUS: *Look for talent.*
Character, too.
Jackie Robinson's
The man for you.
He's got talent
And character, too.
Jackie Robinson's
The man for you!

Narrator: And so Jackie Robinson came to Brooklyn to speak with the general manager about playing on the team.

Branch: Jackie, we like the way you play. You can hit, catch, run — everything! We need good players like you. But I need something much more. I need a man of courage. You will be the first black man to play in the major leagues. Many people won't like that. They're going to make life miserable for you.

Jackie: What do you want me to do? Fight back? I can fight back! I'm a fighter!

Branch: No! No! I don't want you to fight back. I need a man who can be calm, who can take the heat. I need someone who can concentrate when there is shouting and name-calling. Think you can do it?

Jackie: I think so, sir. I'll do my best. My mother taught me that a good man does not fight fire with fire. My mother taught me that the best way to fight is to show how good you are.

Branch: That's exactly right. Show them how good you are. Just play the game and show the fans how good you are! It won't be easy, but I think you can do it.

Jackie: Thank you, sir. I love this game, and I want to play and win more than anything. And I want my family to be proud of me.

Branch: Good luck, Jackie, and welcome to the team.

Jackie: Thank you, sir, and thank you for this opportunity.

Narrator: And at the first game, it was just as expected. Fans booed; they called Jackie terrible names. Even his own teammates avoided him.

Jackie: This is terrible! Why do they hate me so much? I'm so nervous. I hope I don't mess up.

CHORUS: *Be calm, be calm,*
Be very, very calm.
Just play the game.
Just play the game.
Don't talk back.
Don't say a word.
Just play the game.
Don't say a word!

Jackie: Yes, that's it. Concentrate. Block it out. Don't let them get to you. Just play the game. Hit the ball! Catch the ball! Throw the ball! Concentrate!

CHORUS: *Good work, Jackie!*
Good, indeed!
You kept your head.
You kept your word.
You played well.
You played like a winner.

Jackie: Yes, but that was just the first game. Really, I never thought people could be so mean. People even called me to say they wanted to kill me. And would you believe it — I can't stay in the same hotels, or eat in the same restaurants as the other players. I can't believe it!

CHORUS: *Life's not easy;*
Life's not fair!
Life takes courage.
Don't despair!
Don't fight back;
Concentrate.
Play the game;
You're doing great!

Narrator: The booing continued. One game was especially bad. But something unusual happened.

Jackie: The noise is terrible! The booing is awful! Hey, look! Over there! There's Pee Wee. He's coming toward me. I wonder what he wants.

Pee Wee: Hi, buddy, how's it going? Pretty rough out here, isn't it?

Jackie: I can't believe it. They really want me out of here. Even the guys on the team want me out. I can't believe it!

Pee Wee: Listen, Jackie. I don't want you out. Don't even think about it! We're a team. Who cares about the stupid fans who say stupid things? Let's play and win! Let's show them!

Jackie: Thanks, Pee Wee. Thanks a lot. You're a good friend!

Narrator: Then Pee Wee put his arm around Jackie in friendship.

CHORUS: *He put his arm*
Around his friend.
He shook his hand
And smiled again.
The crowd was silent.
What was this?
An act of friendship
On the field.
An act of friendship,
Black and white!

Narrator: And slowly Jackie Robinson was accepted by the public and his teammates. The Brooklyn Dodgers won the league championship that year, and Jackie was named the best new player of the year. He became the first black player to be elected to the Baseball Hall of Fame.

Dr. Salk Saves the Children

Jonas Salk
1914–1995

Jonas Salk was a scientist who, in 1955, developed a vaccine to prevent polio. This disease crippled many children and caused great fear among parents. This play tells about the huge contribution that Dr. Salk made to the health of the children of the world.

Jonas Salk

Dr. Salk Saves the Children

Cast: *Narrator*
Dr. Jonas Salk
Friend
Dr. Salk's mother
Chorus

Narrator: In the early 1940s and 1950s, there was a terrible disease in America. It was poliomyelitis, or polio. It was a children's disease. It left many children crippled. Dr. Jonas Salk was the medical hero who saved the children from this terrible disease. Here is his story.

CHORUS: *Jonas, Jonas,*
What did you do?
How did you save
Our little ones?
How did you save
Our little ones?

Jonas: Well, I was working at the Pittsburgh Medical Center, and I became very interested in viruses. I thought that maybe viruses caused polio. I thought that maybe we could develop a vaccine to prevent this disease. I knew it was important.

CHORUS: *How long, how long,*
How long did it take
To find a cure,
To find a cure
For polio?

Jonas: It took us eight years from the day I began. Eight long years.

CHORUS: *Did you work alone,*
All by yourself?
Did you work alone,
All by yourself?

Jonas: Oh, no. I had a wonderful staff, wonderful researchers, dedicated researchers. They worked with me night and day. Often we worked twenty hours a day, seven days a week. We never thought of giving up.

CHORUS: *What happened then?*
What happened then?
Did you find a cure?
Did you find a cure?

Jonas: Well, it wasn't easy. But finally, after much testing and retesting, we found a cure. I was sure we had found a vaccine to stop polio. I tested it on myself.

CHORUS: *Oh, no! Not on yourself!*
Not on yourself!
Did you really
Test it on yourself?

Narrator: Yes, he did, and on his wife and children, too!

Jonas: Then, on April 12, 1955, we announced it to the people of the world. And as you can imagine, the world rejoiced!

CHORUS: *They honked their horns.*
They rang church bells.
They closed the schools.
They cheered this day!

Jonas: It was wonderful, just wonderful! It really was the best day of my life. I'll never forget it. It was wonderful! No more children with polio!

Narrator: Shortly after this, a friend at the hospital came to Dr. Salk. He wanted to talk about something important.

Friend: Jonas, you have made a wonderful discovery. It is yours. It belongs to you. Perhaps you should apply for a patent. A patent can make you a very rich man.

Jonas: A patent for this vaccine? A patent for something that is for all mankind? A patent to make me a rich man? No, I did not do this to become rich. I did not do it to make money. I did it to save the children. There is more to life than money.

Friend: Well, it's up to you. You could make a lot of money.

CHORUS: *Dr. Salk, Dr. Salk,*
You are good,
And you are kind.
We need more men
Just like you!

Jonas: Thank you, but it's from my parents that I learned these things. They were simple people. They never went to college, but they wanted me to go. They were kind, decent, and generous.

Jonas's mother: We were not well off. We didn't have enough money to send Jonas to college, so he worked after school, and he got some scholarships, too. He was a good boy.

Jonas: That's true. I did work after school. Every dollar helped. My parents always supported me and were proud of me. And now, with this new vaccine, they are even more proud.

CHORUS: *What now? What now,*
Dr. Salk, Dr. Salk?
What will you be?
And what will you do?

Jonas: Well, I don't like fame. I don't like it at all. I don't like to go on television. I just want to do my research. I want to start a research institute. I want to bring together the best scientists in the world and do research.

CHORUS: *Do what you will.*
Do what you will.
But first of all,
Our thanks to you
From all who care,
From parents and
Children everywhere!
Our thanks to you,
Dr. Salk!

Narrator: Dr. Salk made a huge contribution to mankind, a cure for polio. His vaccine stopped the crippling and killing of children. It was an important medical breakthrough.

America's Poet Gets a Call from the Kennedys

Robert Frost
1874–1963

This play is about the life of one of America's most famous poets, Robert Frost. His family life was tragic, but he continued to write poems that Americans love. John F. Kennedy loved his poetry, too, and invited Robert Frost to speak at his inauguration in 1961. It was a special honor for Frost to be the first inaugural poet.

Robert Frost

America's Poet Gets a Call from the Kennedys

Cast: Narrator
Robert Frost
Mrs. Frost
John F. Kennedy
Jackie Kennedy
Chorus

Narrator: Robert Frost was one of America's most famous poets. He was born in California, but moved to Massachusetts when his father died. Robert was eleven. Fifteen years later, Frost and his wife moved to a small farm in New Hampshire. He loved the New England landscape — the fields, the farms, and the hills — and he wrote poems about it.

CHORUS: *Robert Frost,*
Robert Frost!
You wrote poems,
Wonderful poems!

Robert: Well, it's true. I wrote every chance I got. But I had a family to support, a wife and four children. I taught school, and I farmed. I wrote poetry at night after farming all day.

CHORUS: *Is that when you wrote*
Your famous poem?
Is that when you wrote
Your famous poem,
"Mending Wall"?

Robert: Yes. My neighbor and I were fixing the stone wall between our farms. I didn't like fences, but he said, "Good fences make good neighbors."

Narrator: That evening Robert Frost wrote "Mending Wall."

Robert: Something there is that doesn't love a wall …
He is all pine and I am apple orchard.
My apple trees will never get across
And eat the cones under his pines, I tell him.
He only says, "Good fences make good neighbors."

CHORUS: *Walls, walls,*
All kinds of walls.
Fences, fences,
All kinds of fences.
Neighbors, neighbors,
All kinds of neighbors!

Narrator: Life was difficult on the farm. So Robert moved to England with his family. Life was better there. The people loved his poetry, and slowly he became famous. But in 1915, the family had to return to America.

Robert: We have to return to America. War has begun, and it's too dangerous to stay here.

Mrs. Frost: Yes, yes, we should return. We should return quickly! We have to go to a safe place.

CHORUS: *What happened then?*
What happened there?
What happened in
America?

Narrator: Well, he continued to write. He also taught at different colleges. But, tragic things also happened.

Robert: My wife died, and a daughter and son, too. Those were very, very difficult years. Writing helped a little.

CHORUS: *Life was tragic,*
Very, very tragic!

Narrator: John F. Kennedy had always admired the poetry of Robert Frost. He enjoyed reading Frost's poems. He enjoyed reciting them.

Kennedy: That's true. I loved his poems, especially these lines:

> The woods are lovely, dark and deep.
> But I have promises to keep.
> And miles to go before I sleep,
> And miles to go before I sleep.

CHORUS: *The woods are lovely, dark and deep.*
But he has promises to keep.
And miles to go before he sleeps,
And miles to go before he sleeps.

Narrator: In 1960, John F. Kennedy was running for president.

Robert: I do believe Mr. Kennedy would make a very fine president.

Narrator: So, when Kennedy became president, he invited Robert Frost to his inauguration.

Kennedy: Mr. Frost, please come to my inauguration. We would be honored if you would come. Please come and read your poetry. We need poetry for our country.

Robert: Thank you for the invitation. It would be an honor. I accept. It's a proud moment to have poetry in the White House and for the nation. Thank you again.

Kennedy: We are honored, Mr. Frost. It's our honor. And it's time that we bring the arts to the White House.

Jackie Kennedy: Mr. Frost, would you be able to write something new for this special occasion?

Robert: Dear lady, I might not be able to do that, but I can try.

Jackie: Or perhaps you could read one of your other poems. Perhaps you could read "The Gift Outright." It's a beautiful poem. It's a patriotic poem. It's about what America can and will become.

Narrator: On January 20, 1961, Robert Frost came to Washington. He was 86 years old. He recited "The Gift Outright" while the Kennedys and the nation listened.

Robert: The land was ours before we were the land's.
She was our land more than a hundred years
Before we were her people …

Narrator: President Kennedy, Mrs. Kennedy, and all people clapped and cheered. They cheered for America's great poet.

CHORUS: *This land is a gift.*
This land is a gift.
A wonderful,
Wonderful gift!

Champion of Migrant Farm Workers

Cesar Chavez
1927–1993

Cesar Chavez was a hero to the migrant farm workers. Their living conditions were terrible, and they worked very hard for very little money. Chavez organized them into a union in 1962. By using nonviolent strikes, he was able to get an agreement with the farm owners and improve the lives of the farm workers.

Cesar Chavez

Champion of Migrant Farm Workers

Cast: Narrator
Cesar Chavez
Helen Chavez, his wife
Richard, his brother
President Clinton
Chorus

Narrator: Cesar Chavez was a Mexican American who was born in Arizona. He did not have much education — only up to the eighth grade. But he became an important leader. He helped the poor people who worked very, very hard on the farms for only a few dollars a day. He organized the first union of farm workers in the state of California.

CHORUS: *Tell us, tell us.*
Tell us, please.
Tell about your
Early days.

Cesar: Well, I had a happy childhood. We lived in an adobe house where three generations of my family had lived before us. We were poor, but happy. I had a loving family and the great outdoors to play in.

Cesar: Hey, Richard! Let's go gather eggs. Let's feed the horses!

Richard: Yeah! Let's go! Got to do this before school begins! Race you!

CHORUS: *How was school?*
How was school?
Did you like it?
Did you like it much?

Cesar: I hated it. I couldn't speak a word of English because we spoke Spanish at home, and the teacher hated us Mexican kids. If we spoke Spanish, she would hit us. She even changed my name from Cesario to Cesar! Can you believe that?

CHORUS: *What happened then?*
What happened then?

Cesar: Well, our family really hit hard times. It was the Depression, 1939, and we lost our house. My father could not pay taxes on the house, so the government took it over. It was terrible.

Narrator: So, like thousands of Americans, the Chavez family went to California looking for work. They found it on the huge farms of California. They moved from farm to farm, living in shacks and working for pennies a day — parents and children, too.

Cesar: That's when I began thinking: There must be a better way, a better life, a life with dignity. I began to read, to study. A priest gave me a book about Gandhi.

CHORUS: *What did you do?*
What did you do?
Did you speak right out?
Did you speak right out?

Cesar: Oh, no! I was very shy. I didn't like to speak in public. But it made me see the terrible conditions. The grape growers really took advantage of the poor, uneducated people.

CHORUS: *What did you do*
To make things better?
What did you do
To make things better?

Cesar: Well, the first thing I did was to get people registered to vote. Day after day, I knocked on doors. I spoke to the people. Mostly, I listened. They told me their problems. I explained that we needed to vote for new leaders, strong leaders.

Narrator: By 1952, there were four thousand new voters!

Cesar: Then, in 1962, I became the head of the National Farm Workers Association, and we began to have strikes and boycotts against the grape growers. We asked Americans not to buy grapes. We got a lot of support from the American people, and we finally got a good contract, too.

CHORUS: *And slowly, slowly*
Things got better.
Wages were higher
And benefits, too.
Slowly, slowly
Things were better.

Narrator: But the fight was not over.

Cesar: The use of pesticides is wrong — very wrong! Our workers are getting sick and dying. They are being poisoned by chemicals. It has to stop. I've got to do something!

Narrator: And so Cesar Chavez began to fast. He stopped eating. And the world took notice. Letters of support came from all over the world. Some of his workers did not want him to fast. They did not want him to become weak.

Cesar: This is something I have to do. I believe we should sacrifice ourselves for justice. That is very important for me and for our cause. Remember that!

Narrator: After years of fighting, Cesar Chavez died on April 23, 1993. News of his death traveled fast. Crowds gathered at Delano, California, where he had founded the United Farm Workers.

CHORUS: *Thousands came*
From near and far,
Simple farmers,
Migrant workers,
Famous people, too,
To pay their respects,
To pay their respects.

Helen: We held a beautiful memorial service for him. Pope John Paul II sent a special message, and there were thousands of people. It was beautiful.

Narrator: In 1994, Helen Chavez, Cesar's widow, was invited to the White House. President Clinton presented her with the Presidential Freedom Award, in honor of her husband. It is the highest award given to a citizen.

President Mrs. Chavez, in honor of your husband, I want to give you this award. It is a tribute to him and to all the people who work for justice.

The Eagle on the Moon

Astronauts Armstrong, Aldrin, and Collins
July 20, 1969

On July 10, 1969, three American astronauts went to the moon, walked on its surface, and returned to earth. It was an incredible step in the program to explore space. The whole world waited and watched as Neil Armstrong stepped onto the moon and said, "That's one small step for a man, one giant leap for mankind ..."

Astronauts Armstrong, Aldrin, and Collins

The Eagle on the Moon

Cast: *Narrator*
Neil Armstrong
Buzz Aldrin
Mike Collins
Mission Control
President Nixon
Chorus

Narrator: It is July 20, 1969. The world is waiting. Five days ago, three men were sent to the moon: Neil Armstrong, Mike Collins, and Buzz Aldrin. Their mission is to land on the moon today. Will they make it to the moon? Will they return? What will happen? What will they see? What will they do? Let's listen and find out.

Neil: Look, look over there! Right outside the window! There it is! I see it! There's the moon! It's spectacular!

Buzz: Oh, my God! I see it, too! It's huge! It's gray! It's beautiful!

Mike: I can't believe it. It is huge! It's close! Amazing! We've arrived at the moon!

Neil: Listen, guys, I think I hear something. It's Mission Control.

Mission Control: This is Mission Control. You are "go" for lunar landing! You are "go" for lunar landing!

Neil: This is it, guys! We're going to land on the moon. Let's get ready. Buzz, you and I will get into the Eagle. Mike, you stay with the mother ship.

Mike: O.K. Good luck, guys! I'll be watching in case you need some help. I'll pick you up later. Be careful!

CHORUS: *Be careful, be careful,*
Be very, very careful.
The moon has rocks,
Big rocks, small rocks,
Different kinds of rocks.
Careful! Careful!
Do not land
On those rocks!

Buzz: It looks like everything's O.K. for landing … Oh no! We can't land here — too many rocks! We'll crash! What'll we do?

Neil: The automatic control's going to land us on the rocks! We have only ten seconds of fuel left! I'd better take control of this ship!

Buzz: Look! Over there! There's a good place to land — no rocks!

Neil: Right! … O.K.! … Down she goes … Easy does it … Easy does it!

Buzz: Hey! We made it! My God! We made it! The Eagle is actually on the moon!

Narrator: So, with the world watching, worrying, and waiting, Neil Armstrong and Buzz Aldrin landed on the moon in their vehicle, the Eagle. The time was 4:18 P.M.

Mission Control: Congratulations, guys! Congratulations!

CHORUS: *Hooray, hooray!*
The Eagle has landed,
Landed on the moon.
The world is watching.
Men on the Moon!
Men on the Moon!

Neil: Now our mission is to get out and walk on the moon. We'll collect some samples to bring back to earth.

Buzz: Let's do it! You, first. Let's go!

Narrator: So, at 10:56 P.M., Neil Armstrong got out of the Eagle and took the first step onto the moon.

Neil: That's one small step for a man, one giant leap for mankind …

CHORUS: *What did you do*
On the moon,
On the moon?
What did you do
On the moon?

Buzz: Well, first we put up the U.S. flag. Then we stood at attention and saluted it. It was a great moment! After that, we walked around the moon for about two hours and picked up samples to bring back to earth.

Narrator: They also put up a plaque that said:

Here men from planet Earth
first set foot on the moon
July 20, 1969 A.D.
We came in peace
for all mankind.

CHORUS: *How proud, how proud*
All Americans were
To see you there,
To see you there,
To see the flag
On the moon.

President
Nixon: Neil and Buzz, can you hear me? I'm talking to you from the White House. For every American, this has to be the proudest day of our lives … today all the people of the earth are one. May you come back safely.

Neil and
Buzz: Thank you, sir. Thank you very much.

CHORUS: *What a feat!*
What a feat!
You went to the moon.
You walked on the moon.
You all came back.
You all came back!
Thank God, thank God
You all came back!

Expecting
Excellence

Jaime Escalante
1930–

Jaime Escalante came to America from Bolivia in 1964 with no English and no money. He worked hard to become a math teacher in Los Angeles in one of the worst schools in California. He believed that all students, rich and poor, could excel, and, with his own special methods of teaching, his students achieved excellence.

Jaime Escalante

Expecting Excellence

Cast: *Narrator*
Jaime Escalante
High school administrator
High school student
Official from Educational Testing Service
Chorus

Narrator: Jaime Escalante is from Bolivia. He came to Los Angeles, California, in 1964, when he was 34 years old. He had no money and no English.

Jaime: That's true. Oh, I knew a couple of words of English, like "Hello" and "Thank you," but that was about it! And money? No money! No money at all!

CHORUS: *What did you do?*
What did you do
With no money,
With no English?

Jaime: Well, I couldn't get a job. I was a teacher in Bolivia, but I spoke no English and didn't have a California teaching certificate. So, I got a job in a restaurant. I was a busboy.

CHORUS: *He cleaned the tables.*
He washed the dishes,
The dirty, dirty dishes.
He cleaned the floors
In a restaurant!

Narrator: It wasn't a great job, but it paid the bills.

CHORUS: *How did you learn*
The language, the language?
How did you learn
The English language?

Jaime: Well, I went to college. I took English classes and computer classes. It wasn't easy — a new language, a new life — everything was new. Not easy at all!

CHORUS: *But you hung in there.*
You hung in there.
You didn't quit.
You hung in there!

Jaime: Yeah, I hung in there. As I said, it wasn't easy, but finally I graduated from college and got a job as a computer engineer.

Narrator: But his first love was teaching. In 1976 he quit his engineering job and got a job as a computer teacher at Garfield High School in Los Angeles.

Jaime: When I got to school, there were no computers. The school had no computers! How could I teach computers with no computers? So I taught math.

CHORUS: *What was it like,*
Teaching in that school?
How did you like
Teaching in that school?

Jaime: It was awful — terrible at the beginning. The students came from very poor Hispanic families. Their skills were poor. They didn't want to learn. They were undisciplined. Some belonged to gangs. It was one of the worst schools in Los Angeles.

Student: This math is too hard! I don't need math! What do I need math for? I don't want to go to college. I don't need a high school education, either. I don't need an education!

Jaime: So, you want to be a dishwasher all your life! Is that what you want? Is that what you really want?

CHORUS: *And slowly, slowly,*
Very, very slowly,
He changed the class
To a learning class.
One by one
They began to learn!

Narrator: Escalante used his own methods — anything to get his students to learn. He was tough. He was strong. He made them learn. He gave them hope. But most of all, he expected something from them. He expected excellence.

Student: That's right. He did expect a lot. But he gave us hope. He gave us what we call in Spanish *ganas* — passion, desire. We said that word every day in class. He inspired us to do better and better! His class was hard, but it was fun, too.

Narrator: One day, Jaime Escalante had an idea.

Jaime: I want to teach higher math to these students. I want to teach calculus. Then I want them to take a national test to get college credit.

Administrator: That's crazy! These students can't do higher math. These students come from poor families. They have no education. They can't do higher math! They don't even know the basics. They aren't prepared!

Jaime: I'll prepare them. I'll work with them before school, after school, on Saturdays. I know they can do it if they work hard. We have to believe in them!

Admiminis- trator:	All right! All right! Do what you want! But what happens if they fail? They'll feel worse than before. Do you want that?
Jaime:	They won't fail. If they study hard, they will succeed, just like anybody else. I believe they can succeed. If they work, they will succeed.
CHORUS:	*Before school, after school,* *Saturdays, too,* *They studied and sweated* *Calculus!* *They studied and sweated* *Calculus!*
Narrator:	Now the big day had arrived. The students took the Advanced Placement Test.
Jaime:	One by one the results of the test came in. Amazing! Each student passed! Everybody passed! And some with perfect scores! Kids from one of the worst schools in Los Angeles had passed a very difficult test. It was wonderful!
Official:	I'm sorry to tell you this, but we believe that your students cheated on this test. They copied the answers from some- one. These results are not accurate.
Jaime:	What? What do you mean, cheated! My students did not cheat! My students were prepared for this test. They did not cheat!
Testing	But they must have cheated. It's not possible to get such high scores from one of the worst schools in L.A. That's not possible. The students can take the test again if they want to.
Narrator:	So they took the test a second time. And the results were exactly the same. They passed the test with flying colors.

CHORUS: *They passed, they passed.*
They passed again
With flying colors.
They passed the test!

Student: Mr. Escalante was really a great teacher. We loved him. He believed that it didn't matter if you were rich or poor, if you had a big house or lived in the *barrio*. It was your brains and your desire that counted.

Narrator: By 1987, Garfield High School students were fourth in the nation in the Advanced Placement calculus exam. Today, 70 percent of Garfield High School students go to college, thanks to Jaime Escalante, a super teacher.

The Heroes

_____

_____

_____

_____

_____

_____

_____

The Heroes

_____

_____

_____

_____

_____

_____